EXPLORE THE U.S.A.

HAWAI'I

Karen Durrie

LET'S READ
AV2 BY WEIGL
ADDED VALUE · AUDIO VISUAL

www.av2books.com

LET'S READ
AV²
BY WEIGL™
ADDED VALUE • AUDIO VISUAL

Go to **www.av2books.com**, and enter this book's unique code.

BOOK CODE

N641421

AV² by Weigl brings you media enhanced books that support active learning.

AV² provides enriched content that supplements and complements this book. Weigl's AV² books strive to create inspired learning and engage young minds in a total learning experience.

Your AV² Media Enhanced books come alive with...

Audio
Listen to sections of the book read aloud.

Video
Watch informative video clips.

Embedded Weblinks
Gain additional information for research.

Try This!
Complete activities and hands-on experiments.

Key Words
Study vocabulary, and complete a matching word activity.

Quizzes
Test your knowledge.

Slide Show
View images and captions, and prepare a presentation.

... and much, much more!

Published by AV² by Weigl
350 5th Avenue, 59th Floor
New York, NY 10118
Website: www.av2books.com   www.weigl.com

Library of Congress Cataloging-in-Publication Data
Durrie, Karen.
  Hawai'i / Karen Durrie.
    p. cm.
  ISBN 978-1-61913-319-8 (hard cover : alk. paper)
  1. Hawaii--Juvenile literature. I. Title.
  DU623.25.D87 2013
  996.9--dc23
                        2011048027

Printed in the United States of America in North Mankato, Minnesota
1 2 3 4 5 6 7 8 9 16 15 14 13 12

052012
WEP040512

Project Coordinator: Karen Durrie
Art Director: Terry Paulhus

Weigl acknowledges Getty Images as the primary image supplier for this title.

HAWAI'I

Contents

This is Hawai'i.
It is called the Aloha State.
Aloha means "hello."

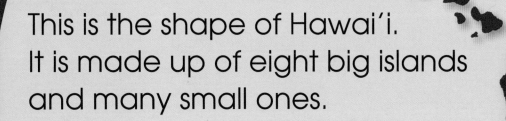

This is the shape of Hawai'i.
It is made up of eight big islands
and many small ones.

Where is Hawai'i?

Hawai'i is in the
Pacific Ocean.

Hawai'i has many volcanoes.
Lava from volcanoes made
the islands. Lava is liquid rock.

Lava can cook a hot dog
in one second.

9

The yellow hibiscus is the Hawai'i state flower. The bushes have new flowers almost every day.

The Hawai'i state seal has a king, a goddess, and a bird.

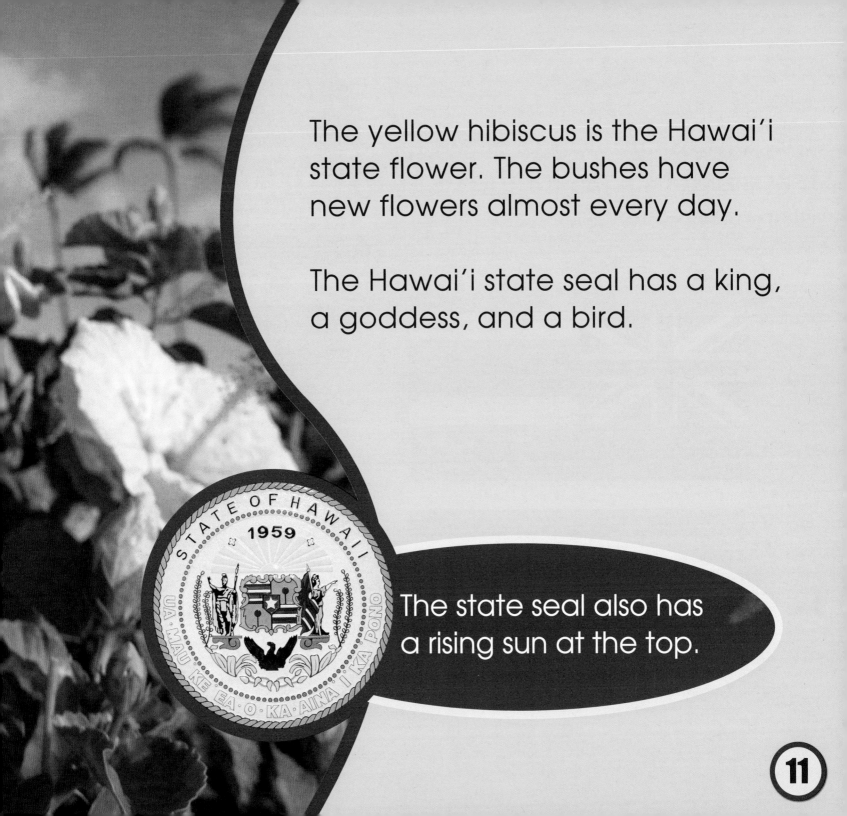

The state seal also has a rising sun at the top.

This is the state flag of Hawai'i. It has eight stripes for the eight islands of Hawai'i.

The Hawai'i flag is red, white, and blue.

The state animal of Hawai'i is the Hawai'ian monk seal. Monk seals are one of the few seals that live in warm water. There are only about 1,400 of them left in the world.

Monk seals like to sleep on the beach.

This is the biggest city in Hawai'i. It is named Honolulu. It is the state capital.

Many ships come to Honolulu.

Pineapples grow in Hawai'i. Hawai'ian pineapples are sold all over the world. A pineapple takes 18 months to grow.

Pineapples are yellow and taste sweet.

Hawai'i is known
for its many beautiful beaches.

People from around the world
come to swim and surf
in the water.

HAWAI'I FACTS

These pages provide detailed information that expands on the interesting facts found in the book. These pages are intended to be used by adults as a learning support to help young readers round out their knowledge of each state in the *Explore the U.S.A.* series.

Pages 4–5

Hawai'i is the only state with two official languages—English and Hawai'ian. *Aloha* is a Hawai'ian word that has other meanings besides "hello." *Aloha* can also mean "love" and "goodbye." Many Hawai'ian islands have Hawai'ian names.

Pages 6–7

On August 21, 1959, Hawai'i became the 50th state to join the United States. It consists of a group of islands in the north central Pacific Ocean. The eight main islands are Hawai'i, Maui, Molokai, Lanai, Oahu, Kauai, Niihau, and Kahoolawe. The state also includes 124 islets. Hawai'i is located about 2,390 miles (3,846 kilometers) west of California.

Pages 8–9

The Hawai'ian islands were formed millions of years ago by lava from giant undersea volcanoes. The main islands are actually the tops of these volcanoes. Hawai'i still has active volcanoes. Enough lava flows from the volcano Kilauea each day to pave 20 miles (32 km) of road.

Pages 10–11

The yellow hibiscus was made the official flower of Hawai'i in 1988. Flowers and plants bloom all year in Hawai'i. The king on the state seal is King Kamehameha the Great. Hawai'i once had a monarchy and was ruled by royalty from 1810 to 1893. The Goddess of Liberty holds the Hawai'ian flag on the right of the seal. The bird is a phoenix, a mythical creature associated with the Sun and fire.

Pages 12–13

In 1816, King Kamehameha the Great had the Hawai'ian flag created. The flag has eight stripes to represent the eight main islands of Hawai'i. It also has the British Union Jack flag in the top corner. Hawai'i had a long friendship with Great Britain. Hawai'i is the only state to feature the Union Jack on its flag.

Pages 14–15

Hawai'ian monk seals are often seen alone or in small groups. They feed on fish, lobsters, octopuses, and eels in the waters near Hawai'i. They go ashore to rest on beaches or find shelter from storms. Hawai'ian monk seals are endangered due to fishing and loss of habitat.

Pages 16–17

Honolulu is the state capital of Hawai'i. The word *Honolulu* means "sheltered harbor." About 375,000 people live in Honolulu. Many ships arrive in the Honolulu Harbor each day. Every year, more than 11 million tons (10 million tonnes) of cargo are brought into the harbor by ship. About 500 cruise ships sail to Hawai'i each year.

Pages 18–19

Pineapple is one of the main crops of Hawai'i. About 185,000 tons (167,829 tonnes) of pineapples are grown in Hawai'i each year. Hawai'ian pineapples are sold all over the world. Pineapple plants bloom about 200 spiky purple and red flowers. These flowers make fruits, which then join together to become a pineapple.

Pages 20–21

Hawai'i has miles of white sand beaches. Waikiki Beach in Honolulu is one of the most famous beaches in the world. Visitors can surf, dive, swim, boat, and even take a submarine tour to see the sights beneath the water. Sea turtles, dolphins, whales, and colorful tropical fish all make their homes in the Pacific Ocean near Hawai'i.

KEY WORDS

Research has shown that as much as 65 percent of all written material published in English is made up of 300 words. These 300 words cannot be taught using pictures or learned by sounding them out. They must be recognized by sight. This book contains 55 common sight words to help young readers improve their reading fluency and comprehension. This book also teaches young readers several important content words, such as proper nouns. These words are paired with pictures to aid in learning and improve understanding.

Page	Sight Words First Appearance
5	is, it, means, state, the, this
7	and, big, in, made, many, of, ones, small, up, where
8	a, can, from, has, second
11	also, almost, at, day, every, have, new
12	for, white
15	about, animal, are, few, left, like, live, on, only, that, them, there, water, world
16	city, come, named, to
19	all, grow, over, takes
20	around, its, people

Page	Content Words First Appearance
5	Aloha, Hawai'i
7	islands, Pacific Ocean, shape
8	hot dog, lava, rock, volcanoes
11	bird, bushes, flower, goddess, hibiscus, king, seal, Sun, top
12	flag, stripes
15	beach, monk seal
16	capital, Honolulu, ships
19	months, pineapples

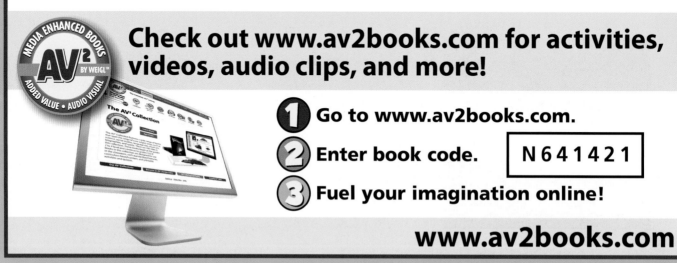

Check out www.av2books.com for activities, videos, audio clips, and more!

1 Go to www.av2books.com.

2 Enter book code. N 6 4 1 4 2 1

3 Fuel your imagination online!

www.av2books.com

24